What Falls Away Is Always

Poems & Conversations

RICHARD TERRILL

HOLY COW! PRESS
Duluth, Minnesota
2020

Author photograph by Linda Tse.
Cover photograph by Jerzy Durczak.
Book and cover design by Anton Khodakovsky.

Printed and bound in the United States.

First printing, Fall, 2020

ISBN 978-1513645636

10 9 8 7 6 5 4 3 2 1

Holy Cow! Press projects are funded in part by grant awards from
the Ben and Jeanne Overman Charitable Trust, the Elmer L. and
Eleanor J. Andersen Foundation, the Lenfestey Family Foundation,
Schwegman Lundberg & Woessner, P.A., and by gifts from gener-
ous individual donors. We are grateful to Springboard for the Arts
for their support as our fiscal sponsor.

Holy Cow! Press books are distributed to the trade by Consortium
Book Sales & Distribution, c/o Ingram Publisher Services, Inc.,
210 American Drive, Jackson, TN 38301.

For inquiries, please write to: *Holy Cow! Press*, Post Office Box 3170,
Mount Royal Station, Duluth, MN 55803
Visit *www.holycowpress.org*

Acknowledgements

Thanks to those who helped out with some of these poems: Bruce Taylor, Kris Bigalk, Christina Olson, Candace Black, Andrew Nye, Christopher Hopkins, Kate MacLam, Marianne Zarzana, Jordan Deveraux, and Lynette Reini-Grandell. Special thanks to Dylan Loring, Michael Torres, and super reader Jenny Fandel, who responded to the manuscript in such thoughtful and helpful detail.

Some of these poems, often in different forms, appeared in the following journals:

American Journal of Poetry: "The New Poetry"

American Literary Review: "Dear Future"

Ascent: "My life is not important...," "Security Question: What Was the Make of Your First Vehicle?," "The Ox and Lamb Kept Time," "Two Sentiments"

Barstow and Grand: "Too Often"

Big Muddy: "Fire at the Fire Station," "10:00 am. Papa's Café, New Hope, Minnesota," "I think I could turn and live with animals"

Brilliant Corners: A Journal of Jazz and Literature: "Chet Baker: A Fantasia"

Cider Press Review: "The Lake," "Early Poems"

Georgia Review: "Coltrane"

Great River Review: "The Verdict"

Hanging Loose: "I'd like please, to leave on your sill...," "Like musical instruments abandoned in a field...," "*Lao Ren*"

Kestrel: "Diane Arbus," "Blossom Dearie Sings and Plays."

New Letters: "Miles Davis Plays 'Stella by Starlight,'" "Roethke at Berkeley, 1967," "What Jazz Isn't"

Qutub Minar Review: "Blackberries"

Volume One: "Next to Nothing," "I'd like please, to leave on your sill..." (reprint), "Miles Davis Plays 'Stella by Starlight'" (reprint)

Contents

In memory of my parents,
who loved music and the natural world

DEAR FUTURE

Apocalittico, dolce

On Edward Hopper

It's not so much
that he's looking at nothing,
but that there is nothing to look at
and we see it too,

a style which purports to show
how gas pumps in a line raise their heads and weak shoulders
above a solitary man in shirt sleeves,

how on Sunday another man can sit on a boardwalk
outside buildings awash in gold. He looks
like an ex-boxer, gartered sleeves,
bald, forearms resting on thighs.

Otherwise, people are extraneous.
Café patrons study their tea cups,
women, nudes, stand looking into severe light
the source of which we may severely

misunderstand. Three mannequins in conference
gather as if human merely because
one of them can kink an arm into a gesture,

and a buxom one can stand so straight that her cupped hands
seem to betray a desire for prayer.
All the other tables, all the sidewalks and the thoroughfare

are not so much empty as filled with space
and with the hoods of monstrous cars. The long backs
of divans, the high roofs and gables,

the black pupils of paired windows
looking out to what must be the sea.

ROETHKE AT BERKELEY, 1967
(T.R. 1907-1963)

He takes carnations from the barrels of guns
to care them back to life,
dances like a bear drowning in the surf,
zigs between guard in their reptilian garb,
—weapons ready, nervous as actors—
and flower children wearing their uniform of rags.

He warns about the napalm from the bat-winged craft,
how it glows like bad calcium in the bones.

But he's most upset
by language, the language
of the silent and of the rest,
of the young and of the armed
—their unexamined verbs
and secret participles. He stands like a ladder
waving against abstraction.

He pokes through the head shops,
tambourines in the cafes.
He thinks he understands
the writhing of the opposed

—the squatters' tents in the campus arboretum,
the afternoon shadows of the soldiers across the quad.

From beyond the hedge,
he watches the police watch
the young pass joints and a bottle of cheap rye.
He can feel the tremor in the earth beneath the street,

but he slumps away puzzled, feet
falling evenly on two and four, the beat
the sun ticks to as it rolls behind the storm.

"I LIKE BORING THINGS"
—Andy Warhol

A few years after graduation I saw my college mentor
at a campus showing of a European art film
—when schools still showed movies like that,
  ones in which a woman disappears just after the opening credits,
  on some island all bare rock in a blue European sea,
  and the other characters abandon
  a perfectly good cocktail party to search for her.

The director wanted to violate
the viewer's expectations
and did it so well, no one
ever stayed awake for one of his films again.

After the show, yawning and ready for the bar,
not yet twenty-five, I told my Professor, much older
it seemed, maybe fifty, that I'd been playing
in an R&B band, staying out all night, reading some,
but more or less wasting my life.

"When you get to be my age," he offered, "you find
you can have wasted part of your life
and not missed much."   Because I believed him,

I kept watching those European movies about painters,
or about composers or writers,
the ones that said more things happen to artists
than ever happen to the rest of us.
Movies that made us feel guilty
for having spent our lives on foolishness.

Chet Baker: A Fantasia

"The Thrill is Gone"

A half-dark moon lights the Tuscan postcard hills,
the postcard narrow streets and villas in Lucca, the old town,
and the walls of the Penitenziario San Giorgio,
where the man behind one of the barred windows plays trumpet, each night,
so purely that the daughters of shop owners, the trattorias' patrons,
even the meter maids and the washerwomen
(even the stray mongrels, even the bricks in the streets)
feel a tide swell and recede in their own personal
longing. The town musicians—*this*
really happened, they'll tell the grandchildren—
gather below his window each morning. *Buon giorno, Chettino,*
they call, and then sing to cheer him. Busted

for shooting up in a gas station restroom,
when the polizia took him off in cuffs, he said,
Man, why are you picking on me?

"My Funny Valentine"

Everybody has a Chet Baker story; I'm the most
honest man I know, and back in '58,
when I used to play the horn and dream,
I met him once outside a club: the movie star
of trumpet. His clothes didn't fit, and one shock of hair
fell across his forehead.

I introduced myself, said I played too, and he said,
Can you loan me five bucks, man?

That night I took the woman who would become my wife
to hear him—a first date. When he played
he was beautiful. I could hear.
But when he sang, I saw her eyes

soften as if everything I wanted were just a lyric in an old song.

What are you thinking now, I asked her.
Why do you want to know, she asked back,
and being who I was then,
and an honest man besides,
I didn't ask again.

"There Will Never Be Another You"

"Ok, you won't be the last girl
I fall for, I mean,
guys write new tunes,
don't they? Different
heads and keep the same
changes? Different words,
but the meaning is timeless—that's love,
I guess. Alfa Romeo

changes their design every season,
and that's why we buy new cars.
'Another fall, another spring,' the song goes.
But only *you* are *you*, aren't you?

We don't say a thrill from one
is the same as the thrill
from all the others. Heartless.
Think of all those different leaves
on all those different trees,
all falling—falling for you, I mean.

I wouldn't lie to you
any more than the next guy:
there will never ever be, never ever be
·(I mean)
another you."

"Look for the Silver Lining"

Whenever he played it all came back
like a puppy off the leash, returning to his master,
like the kite of a boy on a beach,
every day and not just the weekend.

If he played the same interval, the same two notes,
they never sounded the same twice;
If he played a cliché, it wasn't one
since his was an intended forgetfulness, a stop and go

—though mostly go. He engendered illicit sympathy
and too much moonlight. He liked to float around in it.
It was easy for him—I mean everything,
so he didn't think how anything was going to end, and so

it usually didn't. He said,
You want me to tell you the truth,
which only creates pain.
Things like that don't just happen.

DIANE ARBUS

People who think they look like other people

Their disguises fail and the wearer looks
like someone simply trying to look
like someone else. The beard

meant to conjure Lincoln or Fidel,
the cane and bowler hat reminiscent of Churchill
—any resemblance is like the turn in a haiku,
surprising enough for temporary belief.

And what if the person most resembled
used to be famous, and everyone's forgotten?
Who aren't you then? Like a bat in no moon
the opposite of autobiography is starlessness.

Bird legs, warbler flesh, the susurrus rush
around tall buildings in wind—some people
most resemble objects.

One man contending he looked like a bridge
was so convincing that his friends drove over him.
Strangers even stopped to pay a toll.

*

The oldest living dance instructors in America

hurt all over in the morning,
more so than, for instance,
the former oldest living dance instructors in America.

Their slick-clothed stems wobble like stove pipes.
Their shoes fit only on wrong feet.
Steps out of time stagger music into submission.

When they too are gone, the next oldest

dance instructors will still be alive,
but with more panache, more deliberate fancy,
according to their press kit.

Those with a logical mind view birdsong
as simply the tunneling of air
through a bright throat
into indifference, and trees,

while those of a poetic mind
view birdsong as trilled colors,
a dance of possibility

that the oldest living tax accountants
in America, for instance,
could never perform.

Something that was there and no longer is,
is evidence of flight.

*

*Inadvertent double exposure of a self-portrait and images from
Time Square NYC 1957*

"I've always wanted to be in two places at the same time
but living through 1957 once was inadvertent enough.

How many pictures do I have
of that big Philco TV sign
or the flashing COCA COLA
over the teeming intersections?"

*

Mexican dwarf in his hotel room

Why doesn't he have a home, and why
do we assume he's not a Wall Street big shot
or a Cambridge intellectual at a conference in Stockholm?

Everything is out of reach here,
like a Las Vegas of the mind.

Wallace Stevens would have located this very short man
on a wide beach at sunrise,
or in a carriage riding improbably
through some other, unidentified century.

But Diane Arbus finds him in a gray room
with one window on a gray street.
On his improbable smile another window,
which is the camera, which is us.

*

A naked man being a woman

"Let's see, what outfit to wear today...

To uncross my legs crossed at the groin is to
make coffee and hot cereal before Appomattox,
to play in traffic with a joy usually reserved
for the ends of wedding receptions.

The imagination is a wonderful thing
part of the time. On other days
I'll settle for a thin blanket pulled chin high
in a carpetless room, cold like guilt. To expose

my raw turkey parts to someone not me...
so elegant, so intelligent. In photographs,
if I don't breathe, the air doesn't mind.

That photographer lady told me to just be myself, and I paused...

What's left after what one isn't
is taken away
is what one is. I'm the one
who told her that,

and she set the camera aside and
I saw her write it down."

*

Boy stepping off the curb
Loser at a diaper derby
Dominatrix embracing her client

These contact proofs in their chemical darkness
could be framed with graduation pictures
or end up on small bill currency in foreign countries
or posted on a Facebook page with the captions like,
"Winter in the Azores—envy me,"
or "at the Lincoln Memorial—now that's justice."

Masked woman in a wheelchair, Pennsylvania
Boy with a straw hat waiting to march in a pro-war parade
A very young baby

*

The Red rectangle [within the image] represents the way that Diane
cropped and printed it in 1956

There's isn't always some red line
to tell us where to look,
how not to bother with that
which wouldn't bother us
enough.

*

*as if translating images into words were the only way to make them
visible*

The bridge to the island of seeing
is a draw bridge, and the boat traffic
is horrendous. Images
are shaky abutments, words

lie slick on the deck pavement. There is
the crossing and recrossing,
the long commute to perception.
The photos prove

*that something was there and no longer is
like a stain. And the stillness
of them is boggling. You can turn away
but when you come back, they'll still be there looking at you.*

Dear Future

What you think of us will not be your first concern,
just as you were not ours.

You won't know we thought our diligence
would be your salvation,

that we looked out at the trees
and they just stood there.

We each cast a single shadow, longer
at twilight, yes, but soon we couldn't recognize darkness.

Each pin in the map stood for ten thousand
and there were tens of thousands of pins

so we made more maps but found
the world wouldn't grow.

Future, we knew so much for sure
there wasn't room for it all.

Each mind was like a garage so stuffed with belongings
that cars had to park on the streets.

Soon there was simply not enough dignity to go around
or fresh water, which became the same thing.

The very air was like birdsong
we thought we could identify

but the birds knew it not at all, so didn't sing. They couldn't
fly any further south than this.

We thought we could change the subject,
that there were kingdoms yet to come.

We held truth to be self-evident
but it proved to be disguised, difficult

to tease out from our habits and necessities,
which became an embarrassment of exceptions.

The moon itself could be populated. Couldn't it?
The stars bore out our cold abstractions. Down the pipe

always another pagan invention,
each meadow a place on which nothing was built yet.

People grew sadder for what seemed like a long time,
and then they got mad. Future, perhaps you know.

They had come to believe in pure mind
until matter put a cruel end to that short semester.

They never thought that if the wolves roamed too close to the door
their houses had been built too close to the forest.

Future, you became our article of faith,
a proper name, legally changed to rhyme with ours.

If tomorrow as I write is the beginning of you,
the atoms of the days and years between us

may change slowly enough, like failing light,
that you will even think you remember gardens.

"My life is not important. I understand that"
—Robert Dana

Someone spills the deck under the table,
picks up almost every card, and the game goes on.
You couldn't know you'd need that three of spades

to fill your straight an hour later. So it is
you can't draw a line through
what you think is unimportant, and be left neatly

with a few days last February, the snow
almost gone, but the temperature still well
below normal (whatever that means now).

You can be left, though, with the sense that something
is passing daily, hourly, and you just dally
like an apple on a branch. You can be left with your wish

simply to be left alone: you will be,
one day, the house of your life finally quiet.
Pretend the house even now is that calm;

imagine the rain has ended and the porch is almost dry.
Like the dog that's made his rounds about the room
and settled back in the spot from which he rose,

you remember mostly what you can't let go of;
what you have always done you must do again.

"I think I could turn and live with animals"

—Walt Whitman

Life is good, I tell my little dog
and give him his pill for pain and his pill
for the swelling in his spine, and the one

to relax the muscles which are tense I suppose
from not knowing when the pain will come again.
I give him the pill for the blood in his stool

that one of the other pills causes (we don't know which)
so he will feel fine the next morning,
and remember I'm not sure what or how much,

but will want to go for the longer walk
that he would later regret
if I let him walk longer

and if he were able to regret
any joy and the moment and the fine air
and the messages it carries.

Life is good, I tell my little dog,
and I believe, in the moment, he hears and obeys,
so placid and self-contained
I look at him long and long.

The Ox and Lamb Kept Time

Little Drummer Boy

And so it came to pass in those days
that the animals were musical.

Their cloven hooves, caked hard in mud and waste,
could thump a hollow sound at a steady pace
on the barn floor, muted in straw.

They never rushed, never dragged
against the steady progress of their beat,
which was music to the heavens.

It was only human
that the animals' minders and tenders
—shepherds, stable boys—

thought they themselves played the principle instruments,
whether pipes in the field, or the drum of a child
in a song taken to be true.

For the humans in those times, as now,
saw themselves at the celestial center,
a kingdom that rules the kingdom of beasts.

Wise men with gifts, angels on harps and strings
may or may not have been present in the scene
depending on your level of belief.

But the lambs and the oxen? They are unquestionable,
beyond symbol, beyond faith.
It was a barn; we know they were there,

keeping time steady, inalterable,
out of reach of human hands
that shaped and misshaped the very planet

to which all children are born, holy or not,
on that night, or any other.

The carols are wrong. It is the flocks
that kept watch by night,
who by instinct maybe felt a pulse we cannot feel,

and by their presence tell us
we are not the masters.

The Last Thing He Saw

white rhino, male. at extinction

he looked through the bars
where once stood the casual families on sunny days
or men alone poaching long looks
now the doctors naturalists the man
in the khaki who had brought him food and water
all enclosed in the tiny world
they made of the world he knew
being thought incapable of thought
as humans define it
he less than thought
he other than thought
in his gauzy consciousness a picture of water
the rivers he once looked upon bathed in
in dawns with his young
he once raised
his head at birdsong
it's heavy now he has no
soul he is aware of no
need of a soul to be aware
he has no knowledge he is the last
as have the witnesses
the cage of their world like some eternal
miscalculation now proven simply wrong
so a wrong can't last
he doesn't think
alone he can't feel loneliness
like those who keep vigil
feel for him and
someday for themselves
his failing sight
and some glimmer
that something will succeed him
like the thrust of light down
through the canopy of flora
as the poet might describe it
if the poet came to live in those latitudes

The Sense of Things Made Plain

after Stevens' "The Plain Sense of Things"

After the glaciers melted, we returned
to our senses, to things made plain. It was not *as if*
we had come to an end of a civilization;
the inanimate was now having its day, inert in the sun's knowledge.

It was difficult even to choose the adjective
for this stark coda, this gradual crash the madness had caused.
The great structures had become minor,
no distinction—*urban* or *rural*—and less was proven more at last.

The greenhoused world never so badly needed saints.
Spastic efforts had failed repeatedly
—an oily, neglected lesson lent mostly to the flies.

And yet what we couldn't imagine could have been
so easily imagined: a great salt pond
covering the plains, the air's only reflection, leaving
muddy peaks, and water like dirty glass, expressing silence

onto the order of things now sorted out. Rats, a lot of sea,
that wasted pond. All this had eluded,
its inevitable knowledge acquired,
but only when necessity required.

I'm at my favorite dump for breakfast,
usual booth, a stack of today's paper and a pot
of diner coffee—Saturday ritual. On the corner Tv
Fox News calls for another war
with the fervor they used for the last,
but at twice the usual volume.

As patrons leave after breakfast rush
and I still have Variety, Weekend, and Metro/State to browse,
the news cycle rant grows more insistent,
like a bad color painted on bedroom walls
by a previous owner.

The President's waffling, the secretary's complicity,
"boots on the ground" long morphed into dead metaphor
(I imagine so many feet, without legs attached).
How many times can you say the same thing
before someone stops hearing it?
And how loudly? I've never been in such a hurry
to stop relaxing and get back to the stress of the work week.

Then a couple longhairs even nearer to the set
find the remote at the service stand, and simply lower the blast
to a red mumble. Thank you, I say, much too loud now myself,
I've had that lying and crap
rattling my brain all through breakfast. Then I think better:

will some dittohead get up from his eggs to punch my teeth in,
or worse call me out as a wuss
in front of Pam, the nice waitress with all those foster kids,
and the nameless bus boys (who are really men, of course,
and have names, usually in Spanish)?

"It's all money, man," says a young guy in an Autoworld shirt,
"Jerry" in a box above one pocket. "It's the bottom line."

He's right of course. What I'd call class solidarity,
he'd call paying attention.
Then another guy in the farthest booth smiles:
"I could hear it from here. How
did you stand it that long?"

The papers on my table speak silently: rape, abuse,
that war we all wanted. My cakes are cold and the coffee not hot enough,
my biggest problem (*How have I stood it this long?*),
though refills are plenty and free.

When I leave, the streets are still paved.
The cars still go both ways at once,
the clouds still low over the suburbs,
and the traffic lights still signal
yield and caution, stop and go.

THE NEW POETRY

Capriccio vivace

Casablanca: The Stage Directions

A silence falls between them   there is a silence
it grows strained   in even tones

quietly
                sympathetically
                        very quietly

as he draws the shade as they walk
away   as the café is emptying
                                as he pours

in the office
at the bar
in the background
at Lazlo's table, Ilsa sits alone

admiringly
casually
                reproachfully, to Rick
sharply
dryly   steely
                                dead pan
dryly
                shrewdly
harshly

with mock politeness
with intensity
with intense devotion

Rick leaves
Lazlo comes in
        Ilsa rushing in
        the officer exits
Rick and Renault walk off together into the night

barely able to speak
     in a low voice
    his voice low but intense
   trying to keep her voice steady
    in a louder voice
      in French
in French
     inside a swank Paris cafe
  in French

excitedly
    soberly
      loudlysimply

thoughtfully
desperately
    casuallypromptly

  nervously, as Rick pours himself a drink
irritably, to Sam
  respectfully, as he opens the door

bending down
getting up
sitting
beaming with happiness
cutting in   interrupting
shaking his head
  raising his glass
trying to cheer up

to Rick
  to Ferrari
  to an officer entering
    to the cabdriver

                    to Ilsa to Ilsa
to Ilsa and Lazlo
to Ilsa
            to Rick, sighing deeply
            hanging up the receiver and grabbing his cap

chuckling   hardening
half kiddingly, half earnest
tapping his breast pocket
tapping his chest

controlling herself
calling out in French   signaling
the waiter   matter of factly
fondly   morosely
indifferently
in French

    disappointedly
sensing what is coming
    turning back to Ilsa
dashing off and colliding with Karl
    protesting
stiffening
    changing the subject
handing Renault a roll of bills

ill at ease
dazed   distressed

Rick looks at her closely
who has caught the look
                eyes Rick closely
involuntarily, they glance toward   the gambling room
looking at Rick carefully

watching Renault

              Lazlo looks at him, puzzled
a flick of his eyes in the direction of the bazar
shrewdly looking at Ilsa
she looks at him with a vague questioning look
        looks around the empty café
        looks at him directly
        looks at her directly
looking up
looking at his drink
        looking at his glass
looking up from the book
Jan looks at Rick
Rick and the croupier exchange looks

for a moment, a look of admiration comes into Rick's eyes
        glances at Sam
        staring off into space
Rick and Renault watch the plane take off
he looks off and sees Rick
she looks briefly at Rick then turns away

Rick makes a face
        Rick's face reveals nothing
   Rick's eyes react
        his eyes are amused

an amazed credulity is written on Renault's face
facing Lazlo
faces aglow
        their faces are barely visible in the darkness
        his face falling
        Ilsa's face darkens

with a smile

                with a slight smile
                        the implication of a smile
with a wry smile
Ilsa smiles faintly
                smiles
adds, with a smile
                smiles
                smiles just a little
smiling
                smiles
                        smiling insincerely

he smiles and walks off toward the gambling room

Rick smiles slightly and exits toward the bar

Cape Fear

*"The prevailing method in Poland is pseudo-dubbing, where one
announcer speaks loudly over the original soundtrack, reading
the entire script regardless of the age, sex, or emotions of the
character."*
                                    —a website

I'm watching the original back at the hotel, dubbed in Italian
        and broadcast on Polish Tv.
Roberto Mitchum, Gregorio Peck—the Italian's mismatched
        to American lips,

Polsku smothered over the soundtrack like pickle relish on prosciutto,
narration flat as a bureaucrat's memoir.

Martino Balsamini meets Gregor Peczak and hands him a cold one.
Czesc. Grazie, amico. It's closing time at the bistro,

sixty years ago, the band insisting on its three-chord message,
and Mitchum now centered in the frame. (How like

the *tavernski* from which I've just returned, near the gates
of the Old City, with its shadows and angles, perpetually
        under renovation.)

Bob eyes a redhead (the film is black and white),
her hairdo puffed and stuck, brows sharp enough to break skin,

Mitchum the only one in the film who speaks American,
her will reduced to the foam on his beer: *"Baby, I just don't care...."*

Chest of a peasant, striped shirt like a gondolier,
wavy hair like somebody's Uncle Cliff before the war.

Later, he eyes Peck's nubile daughter and crushes another beer can, says
something no Pole would say, or an Italian might, but to a much
        older girl.

Becoming Groucho

> *"Groucho was depressed because he was the only one in the*
> *world without a Groucho Marx to cheer him up."*
> —*Dick Cavett*

our coattails split and flap like bat wings
our hollow notes whistle like old robin song

we do a little dance, this way and that like a cock
our feet sweeping circles in the air near the floor,

in fact as soon as I met you I swept you off my feet
clockwise, counterclockwise, wise guys double jointed at the knees

they think I look alike, that's a tough break for both of us,
my painted mustache brushed on you, I want to brush up on my Greek

so go find a Greek and brush up on him
between the two of us we'll solve this poem

especially if you go home, but don't go
for you have beauty, charm, money

(you have got money, haven't you?), don't go, Julius, Professor
oh Captain my Spaulding, Senor Novelli's first selection

will be somewhere my love lies sleeping with a male choir
the next number is a flute solo, which we'll skip

and dance the Charleston in a glassless mirror
in bare feet and night*shoits*, hopping like rabbits

the overnight train leaves for vaudeville early
in the last century, but don't go, I'd buy you a parachute

if I knew it wouldn't open
I'd rent you out as a decoy for duck hunters, why don't you

cross at the corner when the lights are against you
why don't you just lie down until rigor mortis happens

there's not room in this john for both of us, so let me out, let me out
or send in a magazine, just don't go. I was to be the one

whistling on the set, left holding the phone, hello?
I may be wonderful, but I think you're wrong

Chico off to the track, Harpo home to his noisy kids
I was the one who'd get you the beautiful young *goils*

get you the lunch date with T.S. Eliot
a seat at the table with Bertrand Russell, hello

you were the only one in the world
without a Groucho to cheer him up, no more! hello!

we'll call for the president's car
and sit on each other's lap

we three could make a beautiful couple
so don't go, hello

hello
hello

this leaves me speechless
and see that you remain that way

stay a week or two
stay the summer through

but still I'm telling you
I must be going

(and not a *woid* about to this to anyone
not even me)

"Fans, don't fail to miss tomorrow's game"
—Dizzy Dean

Otherwise
you may be in the stands   alone
since this broadcast reaches a wide audience
if tomorrow comes
as scheduled
no athletes will leave their caps on
during an anthem that won't be played
the flag that won't be flying
may lack both stars and stripes
it will be the opposite
of extra innings less
than rain shortened
no zeroes will be
affixed to the centerfield scoreboard
above the green ivy that will still grow
in lovely entanglement with the afternoon sun
no promotions no giveaways but
the overpriced hot dogs will be
as good
as free
if you can find
                            a vendor
the beer would flow
past the seventh inning curfew
if your thirst for it hadn't stayed   away
like everyone else who
listened to this broadcast
(which reached a wide audience)
baseball so much like life
benchwarming at the end of the dugout
stealing signs
left stranded in scoring position
sacrifice
optioned to triple A
l o n g periods of inaction

broken
by ! drama !
that's usually
        unproductive
so much like life
that for tomorrow's game
you even know the final score

You write it the way
you sign someone else's name.
You read it the way
you read a menu in a foreign language
you could be fluent in someday
if you don't lose your appetite.

It's in the ash tray your uncle brought back from the war:
"Belgique, 1945" the lettering reads
below a replica of *Manneken Pis,*
a small brass boy who tinkles onto snubbed butts.

It's in the small octagonal mirror with gilt frame
the Chinese hang opposite doorways
to ward off evil spirits as they enter the room.

The new poetry thinks itself
impervious to light, to flame, to drowning.
It resides wholly between silences. Even
when death's advance team schedules a meeting,

the new poetry chatters on,
changing lanes at the intersection,
changing tense mid-thought,
making change with the homeless vet at the exit ramp.

Its best lines are souvenirs
of vacations you would never pay to take.

It plays sincerity well, if rarely, a few notes
folded in with the many-colored laundry.
A voice within the voice.
Socked feet warm along the wood floor.

The new poetry looks mostly without,
seldom within. It says everything
must change, yes. But from what
to what?

Daily News/Paper Sh r e dd e   r

A photo, circa 1873, shows a man

                                        without
                his legs and
                low
                        er

        arms we tend to   project

our own feelings
on the situations of others
I can get 50%
                                off trays coasters place mats

but only through a week

from Wednesday in Sleepy Eye Minnesota

                        there is a little girl
                        in constant pain skin
                        so delicate that each night when
                        her parents remove her bandages she cries

                *[In the obits, the average age at which people die
                        is still older than I am!]*

and no
drug, no
cure can
bring relief   breaking
                        in police found a fold out couch
                        in the crowded living room and a kitchen

        piled
        high

with
the
unwashed
at Dingo's bar

      though one man called him a friend "but now
      I realize I didn't understand George at all" a gunman

was wounded in a parking lot a mother
poisoned her infant child

              [I no longer
        know the names in Famous Birthdays]

High
      of 62

   in the upper forties
low   "I argued

with George time and again
to get out of that apartment and
spend his money and enjoy life" free
vein screening November 7 I can
avoid spinal surgery do my shoes
fit right warming up again rain
in sight "he never
went to restaurants embarrassed
that he needed three entrees to be
satisfied" a man named George
Bell died and no one
found his body for days
unseasonable
        ["One thing about George,
          he didn't get personal."]

what you always
did don't do
write with the wrong
hand
write with the left
side of the brain

breast stroke not side
schubert not brahms

play the changes
for a change
listen to the piano
not the bass
skip the extra chorus

requite love
death's a hunch
start over
skip lunch

ignore the voices
you first heard long ago
telling you someone else
got more than you
someone else got better

that nightly scotch
make it two or none
make it bourbon or gin
don't begin
anything you can't finish

you who always changed each line
you who always changed
each line you

who never finished anything

Haiku Bumper Stickers

it's Unhappy Hour:
drinks one for the price of two
all bar snacks marked up

on the mountain top
look back to the valley where
the steep climb began

opening a new
jazz club why don't you just burn
thousand-dollar bills?

the moon is a crust
of bread a crust of bread will
never be the moon

being lonely is
good religion the church closed
for renovation

the cicadas hum,
the gray shush of the neighbor's
air conditioning

if fate co-authors
your life what did it write what
did you? And the end?

the ocean is what
the rain would do if it weren't
so busy falling

with the sun lower
like a shadow underground

the darkness rises

fifty percent chance
of just about anything
not reassuring

the world raises its
black flag in surrender no
one told it the rules

Wagner never wrote
a symphony Coltrane a
string quartet, Chopin
a good Broadway musical
you really can't blame them though

drinking beer is like
a bad sestina: same words
and not much to say

when no one sees me
I grow used to my absence
did you say something?

our lives don't really
matter much but we must live
them as if they do

smallest bird at the
feeder the beak of that bird,
the seed in its beak
the husk of that seed fallen
to the ground before the snow

silence makes little
sense but how much sense do you
need? how much silence?

honk if you love this

The Villanelle is Hard to Master

The art of complaining isn't hard to master.
So many things seem worthy of contempt
mere honesty about them is no disaster.

Be grumpy every day, don't just *accept* the fluster
of cheery co-workers, vying to become saints.
The art of gossip isn't hard to master.

Then practice bitching louder, breaking plaster,
cursing names, outrageous bills, the soaring rent.
Don't try to make cashmere what's polyester.

The guy who gloats about Trump? Clock the bastard.
Even your ex-therapist said it's good to vent.
The art of violence isn't hard to master.

If people don't like it, who gives a piaster?
It's your life taking on water, so don't relent.
To breech the dam of restraint brings someone else disaster.

Even pissing off you, reader, with my one-fingered gesture....
Hey, I've presented sound evidence:
the art of complaining's not too hard to master.
Never give up? Screw it—life's a disaster.

> "It is difficult to understand how Pteranodon stood on land.
> Probably it propped its body off the ground by resting on its
> knuckles."
>
> —*The Hot-Blooded Dinosaurs*

He flies over tar pits, Cretaceous oceans
and lands gracefully at the local saloon,
where dinosaurs network and crocodiles congregate,
pre-beings howl at what will be the moon.

Bat-bird or dragon man? Flying marsupial?
Swimmer in ancient seas? Just plain nice guy?
Paleontologists couldn't agree if his
winged finger meant he got mud in his eye.

Marvelous endotherm! High-order vertebrate!
So unreptilian! So debonair!
Gentle intelligent, intricate pterosaur
spent his adult life all gliding in air.

Only the ground ever gave him a problem.
He rests on his knuckles and sips on his drink.
For dinosaurs are a convenient reminder that
someday the rest of us will be extinct.

"No one should write their memoirs until after they're dead"

—Samuel Goldwyn

That's a little harsh, but with the hindsight of the grave,
your mother's shoplifting, your father's girlfriends,

the last great war and all the little wars tagging along,
the stray bullets in the tough parts of town

that find toddlers playing in their front yards
—all may start to coalesce into a paraphrasable *something*.

Why write it down in life and risk misunderstanding,
and no end to the narrative arc besides? As for

your own minor longing, table-grade dissatisfaction,
garden-variety loneliness: the three marriages,

the prosthetic heart, the *etcetera*?
Just leave them in boxes under the stairs to be found or not
        by descendants,

your epitaph to carry one last good joke: "*it was not as bad
as he thought it was going to be.*"

The catch is, I guess, you have to be alive
to do the marketing of whatever book you write,

and if you can't market your life,
you sold your soul for a lot less

than you could have gotten for it.

"PISSING IN THE SNOW OUTSIDE MY DOOR—IT MAKES A VERY STRAIGHT HOLE"

—Kobayashi Issa

For years I took the dog out at bedtime
—his and mine—so he could lift a leg
(always the right hind leg, I noticed)
on the neighbor's Japanese peony
or in winter on the pile of crusted snow
along the driveway.

One evening I thought, why should I go in and have to flush?
The moon some nights glows so,
I can't be mad at her.
And in January the cold
is always the same—like when I was a kid
and we were going inside for hot chocolate,
clothes soaked through from play.
The dye from yarn stained my blond temples red
under my stocking cap (Wait, I'll show you, still,..).

Tonight, I enjoy the advantage of the much-maligned burbs:
my street one block long,
neighbors all deaf or retired, in bed for hours,
I can water their perennials, even mid-winter as they sleep.
I can piss straight
outside my door. The dog doesn't care,
just looks at me and sniffs on in the dark.

"Moaning helps. It doesn't ease the pain, but it lets you know that
someone cares, even if it's only you.
Moaning also lets you know you are still alive."
                        —*Mike Royko, "How to Cure a Hangover"*

I've probably told you this story before, but there used to be this
bar on the north side of Chicago called the Jury Room. I guess you were
supposed to order a round, elect a foreman, and render a verdict on the
day's events: guilty, guilty, guilty.

You could fight about who gets to be smooth-faced Henry Fonda, and
who has to be cranky Lee J. Cobb in the movie version of *Twelve Angry
Men* (which we studied in eighth grade, by the way), and who has to be
nervous young Jack Klugman—I was surprised the other day to read he
had only just died, maybe the last one in the cast to pass. *Yeah*, I thought,
the movie's that old.

But the Jury Room—it was this very average watering hole with this
great front window with a bar rail and row of stools right below it. You
could look up and the whole world was your bartender—the way it should
be, we thought then.

The street was Lincoln Avenue, twenty hundred something, and the
window looked out at yuppie designer clothing stores (yuppie cause this
was the 1980s, I can't remember just when), and women's resale shops,
and stores selling plastic molded furniture or organic futons for your
apartment, maybe even a dentist office or a Montessori school.

The El ran by on Fullerton, almost out of ear shot, and the
neighborhood was already prettified with refurbished three-unit
brownstones, which now nobody could afford to rent— petunias in
decorative wooden planters, beveled and carved, and varnished wood
doors (like in some English manor in the movies). And a concrete stoop—
about the only thing that wasn't wood except for the brownstone. And
the petunias.

I say *petunias*, but this story takes place in winter. Prominent in the
view from the Jury Room window (may your sentence be a thousand years
of happiness—is that from a fortune cookie, or some William Holden
movie about the Qing dynasty? Ha!)—right in front of your pint of lager
was the Biograph Theater, its marquee lit up like a thousand restroom

mirrors, only better in the snowy night. The bulbs popped on and off in that snake of illumination, like corpuscles moving down some visible artery. At the window you could almost smell the popcorn across the street—except what you were smelling was the stale kernels in the machine in the back of the bar, empty since happy hour (maybe empty since a happy hour in about 1962).

The Biograph Theater was where they shot John Dillinger, in the alley just to the side of it. He had been watching *Manhattan Melodrama* with Clark Gable, but everybody knows that. I've never seen *Manhattan Melodrama* myself—some gritty crime story with a then-and-now plot, somebody showing poor judgment in a life of crime—but it was old J.D.'s last feature, and they gunned him down running away, or maybe he turned and shot back, I can't remember.

"All right, Rocky, we know you're in there, come out with your hands up."

"You'll have to take me out by the heels, copper."

"It's curtains for you, Rocky. Curtains." That kind of thing.

There's a plaque on the side of the theater now telling you what really happened. Some people say Dillinger's ghost lingers there as well, but I don't buy it. Why would the ghost of a glamorous guy who made a fortune by illicit means hang out in an alleyway? If you want you can go to the alley and judge for yourself. But you can't make out that plaque from the window of the Jury Room—much less some ghost, not in the snow anyway.

I say *snow* because, remember, despite my telling you about the petunias, this was winter. I'm sitting in the window of the Jury Room on Lincoln Avenue, the snow is swirling down and around—wet, heavy flakes, like there's pieces of Lake Michigan in each of them. The lights of the marquee are doing their snake dance, even though the late feature's probably out by now. The street is deserted—like at the end of some apocalyptic sci fi flick from the fifties. From the bar, you can see the cold outside; from these seats by the picture window, you can feel the draft.

And amidst this picture of kitsch and yuppie life, winter and the Biograph Theater, the allergist's office (second floor) and the tableware boutique, there's one liquor store in the neighborhood, right next to the Theater. It's the only place in view that's still open this late. The lights there never go dim, it seems, and they bleed out weakly, reflected in the slush in the street.

So we're sitting there staring into the weather like dying stars, and one guy walks out of the door of the liquor store, pulls his coat collar up and his scarf around his neck against the cold. He's wearing one of those caps like guys wore in movies in the 1930s, and he pulls it down low over his forehead, so only a patch of his face is exposed, and that patch is covered by a big pair of dark framed glasses.

"Hey," somebody says from the window railing. "That's Mike Royko!"

And Jesus, it was. Everybody laughed. The figure clutched a single brown paper bag the size that would hold a pint of something. He jay walked across Lincoln Avenue, off the curb in front of the liquor store, diagonally through the Chicago slop in the street in front of the Theater, and directly toward the window of the Jury Room bar, where we had been sequestered to perform our civic duty that winter night.

Right when he got to our side of the street, Mike Royko paused for a moment, then instead of heading for the entryway of the bar, he veered northwest on Lincoln Avenue, showing better judgment on a night like this—as far as we could tell, never to return.

The laughter subsided quickly, a hush fell and nearly hurt itself, then everyone went back to his deliberation. We agreed that if the weather had been anything but awful, Mike Royko would have joined us for a drink. But after all, who'd sit in a bar on a night like this?

It's not the story's
truth, but its weight in weather
fills streets with snow.

this brings us roundabout to the question of why
this brings us to the double-spaced guitar
the spell-checked tarantella, the boy carried off
in the wind's arms, the sun a kite in rain

this brings us to biography and farce
to failing sight, a road to now in snow
a side trip to the Plain of Jars, a horn
that sounds across collapsing skies

which of these items doesn't belong?

when a sentence ends, an angel has departed
or so the linguists mutter over coffee
before a thought can form, it mucks about
in our genitals and the culture of our ancestors
or so the theorists insist

before the grand design of what's left of grace
we stand skeptical if not appalled. Truth
no less threatening than shrapnel in the heart,
no less a shadow than a lethal tambourine

"I'D LIKE, PLEASE..."

Non troppo sentimentale

"I'D LIKE, PLEASE, TO LEAVE ON YOUR SILL JUST ONE COLD FLOWER
WHOSE BEAUTY WOULD LEAVE YOU INCONSOLABLE ALL DAY"
                —*Jon Anderson*

In hindsight what you longed for
seems part of some canon,
items on a list everyone
was supposed to have wanted.

Or like a scene from a silent movie
screened in a noisy bar
crowded with people younger than you
intent on something you don't remember
the particulars of. It is as if

that disease of longing
was judged incurable
by the medical panel at the Institute,
then the doctors all died
while all the test patients outlived them
by ten or twenty years.

You don't mind.
For gradually, at around fifty maybe,
when your narcissistic worry
about love
morphed into a narcissistic
awareness of death,

there came the sense that something
had already passed, without passing
in sight. Like a train
the sound of which on still nights
conjures the whole of travel, the

speed and freight danger along tracks,
through the shoddy woods and through the bad
parts of town, closed factories with

shattered window glass, a here
and an elsewhere, and no matter
which is which.

"The scent of smoldering leaves, the wail of steamers.
Two lovers in the park who walk like dreamers"
— *"These Foolish Things (Remind Me of You)"*

It's always playing somewhere:
It's playing on a pier in a distant capital,
and in a bar where you're still allowed to smoke
—almost required to, in fact. It's playing on a movie soundtrack,
tagging along with the image at the edge of the celluloid
like Christmas lights along the gables. It's playing
on "a tinkling piano in the next apartment,
those stumbling words that told you what my heart meant."

On the foolish list are the things we treasure
because we know we shouldn't, because we fear
that someday we'll forget: the cadence of a lover's breath,
or the way fall feels in a park in the rain. Forget
and we're left only with what's happening now,
which should feel important, but doesn't.
"Oh, how the ghost of you clings," or so we hope.

I wonder why lovers dream in songs and we sigh,
whereas in the waking life dreaming means
wanting something that likely will never come,
like justice or a better job, and in sleep
dreams make sense so seldom that people
just chuckle about them at breakfast.

It's always raining in October. Far
from any seashore, gray is not a color,
not a blanket, but a silence you could drink.
It's always chilly in the park. That's why
nobody's here and it's such a good place to go.

Please tell me your name again.

"LIKE MUSICAL INSTRUMENTS ABANDONED IN A FIELD
THE PARTS OF YOUR FEELINGS ARE STARTING TO KNOW A QUIET"
—*Tom Clark*

Sadness has toned it down, joy
has clammed up entirely,
longing is starting
to keep things a little more to herself.

The field in question is timothy grass,
wild raspberry taking over
along the edge that gets the most sun.

There might be a few poplar shoots
reminding us this meadow will be seedlings
long before it's a repository
for love, anger, grief, or indifference.

It's a shame only about those instruments left behind.
Some poor kids could be playing them in the school band....
Ok, I know the poet is just making metaphor,

which is a kind of joke for smart people.
Indifference is not a bass clarinet,
weeping is not a cymbal crash,
anger isn't scored for brass, as right as that sounds,

and love, that snob,
pretends it's too good for any music
we could make.

Fire at the Fire Station

The checkerboards upended, the tv ballgame shorted out,
    black coffee spilled,
the Dalmatian with the red neckerchief jumps upon engine number 4,
then back to the pavement, puzzled, and waiting for a lead.

Tongues of smoke lick the golden pole through the hole in the floor
up to the cots where firemen doze; flames gather,
looking strangely blue. Nothing is as it should be.

The clang of the alarm: *red red red.*
And the men don their thick slickers and hats,
and look to each other,

not knowing whom to call. They're not men
given to introspection, given to consider
the kind of irony that shows up in newspaper accounts

the next morning. And the three-year-old boy
on the sidewalk, pointing to the first signs of contradiction,
the ash rising from those red brick garages all in a row,

would be me, holding my grandfather's hand. I don't
remember exactly, but we probably
came to see the giant trucks and ladders,

even the tires polished to shine. Perhaps,
while we watched, an alarm somewhere would be thrown
and the rescue would set out, all ablaze with motion and danger.

SECURITY QUESTION:
WHAT WAS THE MAKE OF YOUR FIRST VEHICLE?

When I was 24, my father insisted it was time I finally owned a car.
He gave me his sky-blue Ford LTD, the car my mother had driven to
work to be greeted each morning by a young colleague who hailed,
"Look, here she comes in the Queen Mary." Now, nine years of miles
under its frayed belts, its old hoses were spilling their essence on
expressways miles from home, leaving me at the mercy of small-town
mechanics with big dreams.

With a travelling job, it was time I owned a used car I'd bought
myself. I carshopped with Dad, who knew the ropes, and we ended
up at a dealer, an uncle of a man my father knew slightly at work.
And there it was: A Ford LTD, the next year's model from the one he'd
given me, or maybe the year after that. Different color—Executive
Tan—but same white vinyl top. They'd changed the chrome, Dad
pointed out.

The next day I drove home by myself in a used Toyota Corolla, forest
green, five on the floor. Its engine hummed like a happy aircraft. I
drove it past the years, until I saw road beneath the floorboard, and
then more.

But that day I drove it off the lot, to my father's home now, my father
said nothing. No Jap jokes, no "less car more money," no worry
about the scant availability of parts. That was wisdom, perhaps love.

So how should this poem end?
With the paragraph preceding?
Or with another leading
down another road,
the world changed again
in color, size, and pace
and I am that man standing old,
bemused, unminded in the driveway,
without sons or their complications
to temper my regret? My dismay
at watching all the different models race
to their different, newer destinations?

Remember How Great

those old poems that friends
wrote on bar napkins
about women in bars or about fathers
they described as stern and distant
but who were probably just busy
with their own disappointments

poetry could be about something
the dance or wandering lonely as a cloud
dead precedents or sparrows along a hedgerow
your uncle with the glass eye
even though he never had one
your aunt who gave the bad piano lessons
which is why you never learned did you

now you feel only
that you'd like a little snack
too close to bedtime
or that the glow from the last light
in the afternoon at quarter after four
means that another day has passed
without a lot of change
in weather you can point to
and that it's winter again like yesterday

true there's leftover carryout in the fridge
an earlier portion of which
interested not even the dog
he sleeps still in his cozy bed
near the unlit fireplace the bed
which smells so much like him to him
that he sometimes thinks he's part of it
or so it seems to you

The images are like old friends
I no longer have enough in common with.

"Three-sweatered like a crusted pine,"
"The fisherman scent of imagined waves,"
"He shakes his cock like a tired flag."

I pretend I wouldn't recognize them
on a dark street, even with a gang

of marching nationalist editors
gaining on me from behind,
red pencils sharpened to pin accuracy.

And it was always night in these young poems
—"night is evening's secret,"
"a myth about a night world,"
"we wait for night and night-

feeding bass"—as if daylight
were owned by prose

and of little interest
mostly because
there was no bourbon in it.

And what did the young man know about love
—"too simple for listeners; too difficult for art"—
that now he wouldn't cut back

until the part about how hard it is
was left to extend its bare branch
into the winter sky?

LAO REN

Slowly, smoothly, slowly,
as if pushing and pulling the very air
we were once born into,
we're coming out of Snake Striking in the Long Grass
when Zhang, my usually-silent Tai Qi master, quips,

If you stay in that Pilates class
you will have "six abs"
and impress all the ladies.

We flow seamless into Repulse Monkey.
I step back three paces
and gingerly pause.

Susan the pretty Chinese pharmacist,
maybe fifty something,
is missing today,
so is Nihad the Bosnian astrophysicist
of indeterminate age.
It's just the old guys—both of us—

so even Master can be chatty
and still bend deeply at the knees,
to sweat more completely.

He makes the *qi* jump like current
from palm to palm in Play the Pipa
also known as Break Your Opponent's Arm.

Have you seen a commercial,
the man our age,
with the tight stomach,
always standing with some pretty lady.
Just eat his pills and—magic!

We Pat the Horse's Tail
and our White Crane Spreads Its Wings
over the fieldhouse concourse
on which administrative assistants
take their lunch hour walking laps.

"But you and I?" Master posits.
Testosterone?
Zero!"

I laugh, to say nothing, about to go
into our last and highest kick
and then into the right and ready pose I call
Don't Fuck With Me
—left arm guarding, right arm cocked back

as if to warn some unwary combatant
of the weaponry of pure experience.

Too Often

You write too often
in the elegiac mode

he said, making coffee
and French toast holding

an infant in one arm
and generally tidying up

the kitchen with the other
hand. *I've told you this*

more than once.
And while I sat waiting

for breakfast I knew
he was right but not

what to do about it. Now
the child grown, the dishes long

pushed aside, he has all but lost
the gift of speech, so that I

put my ear to his lips,
both his hands covered

by a wrap in his chair.
I can make out only air

in short motion, less than
syllables, less than

breath almost. Less. He's
repeating their pattern

the same puffs
twice, a third time

but I've lost the gift
to write too often

and the patience
to listen

and don't know what
to do about it.

Miles Davis Plays "Stella by Starlight"

And why not, I say, on a rainy afternoon like this,
cold in the basement, too warm upstairs,
when his high notes cut like rays through cloudshine,
his mute another reason not to say anything.
You know this tune, you poetic

jazzer wannabes: you late-
middle-aged guys cueing up Coltrane
coming in for his chorus on vinyl—mid-era Coltrane
with his runs to the plaintive high wail,
his ghost notes incarnate a fifth lower than the melody's trail.

It's been sixty years since that studio date and "Stella" still
        swings easy
like premium gas or next Sunday with the top down.
May we all articulate such grace in our fondest wish, our most
        desperate
crying jag held inside, as we practice to be older women and men.
Bowed bass and the piano rubato take us to the end.

For this is good vinyl—darker, bolder even than the dark modes
to come for Miles and his brethren an album or two hence.
May we open our senses, heads unbowed.
May we drop the needle on 1958 one more time.
We were all alive then, weren't we?

What Jazz Isn't

Warm nights with the shades drawn and windows open,
an elegant dinner with a ladyfriend in a cocktail dress,
a world of people doing the lindy hop in zoot suits,

or slick guys on street corners ducking cops, pimping downtime.
Nor is it shared needles or double highballs
and all-night bashes—not *only* that, at least.

None of that movie fill about angry young men
going further out at midnight—always midnight,
as if jazz musicians never went to bed early during the week,

never mowed the lawn or bought certificates of deposit.
As if they weren't bored like you and me most times.
As if they all wore funny hats. Once

jazz was simply something with other people
you couldn't do alone. It was good metaphor like good wine,
or an idea like waves on clear days.

It was the abstract neo-pre-modern *something*,
only in scales and chords. Or playing sides with other guys
who understood—*cats*, if you must.

What is jazz now? As Chairman Mao said
about the French revolution,
it's too soon to tell. Will it become again

some new animal, eyes shining in the dark,
the thing you least expect
could survive on such lean pickings, the thing you most

can't name without giving it away?

touch the keys so lightly
you'd think light would rise
instead of shine

and the patrons willing through it all
to pay attention to her voice so small
and so in tune it can easily fit
between dust and dust jackets
motes and liner notes

shouldn't all jazz waltzes
be in b minor?
aren't all smiles
quiet smiles?

listeners look for a rhyme with experience
Blossom Dearie sings to her audience

(like something about to close
for the season that makes you
want to wish for spring again)

rhyme trees with hive of bees
hung with got stung and, of course,
with young, as in, the past
the only thing she means
the only thing that lasts

If I were a phone you'd answer
If I were a song bird you'd sing.
If I were a week or a month
time would oh go by

elusive celebration
momentary permanence
absolutely temporary
bicarbonate of romance

(that trill on a final note
whenever it's evening)

and if she should misbehave?
moonlight savings time!
her range your range
her made-up heart, yours too

I'm no theoretician
but in a good position
to be a jazz musician
hope it's no imposition

(*the next song will be a sad song*
again oh again
life so beautiful
you'll miss your train)

COLTRANE

he liked to laugh
didn't smile on album covers
only because
his teeth were bad

once there were so many
waiting in line he took
tickets at his own gig
so the doorman could
catch a break to pee

he was shy and if you weren't
he just agreed with you
journalists came away
writing about themselves

he said *sometimes*
I wish I could walk
up to my music as if
I had never heard it before

he asked *did you*
like it did you really
think
I played well

imagine him
among the galaxies like light
bending gently through time
(Einstein knew
about that early but
kept it to himself)

or imagine him earthbound
breathing the very air
you later would

then see him instead almost
ninety tending his garden
hoeing red potatoes
sweet as kept promises

dragging his rusted implements
lacquer worn away to essential
beauty gently
over the loose soil

which is also sweet
to the small animals
living there and who can hear
him hum
in the chords'
upper structure

see him, maybe,
leave the yard
still too soon
as if it didn't matter
as if all the world weren't there

Two Sentiments

Resisting Irony

Oh heart, if I passed you on the street you would not stop
and neither would I. I would
note your bruised clothes, the slow
movements pulsing from your chin and hairline,
your failing red. But I would not
offer alms or a warm hand. Is this
cowardice? Fear of getting involved?   Perhaps
I would meet your glance only at the moment we passed
—to profess my small music, which is sympathy.

But I would speak only to myself: there but by grace
goes some organ or appendage more necessary,
like the stomach or the tired feet.

Against Depression

Long live red pick-up trucks and fancy dancing,
hot tips, barbecued ribs, 1950s sci-fi flicks,
bobble head afternoons and out of the box bantering.

Here's to the top of the batting order,
drinking from the bottle, losing battles,
getting better. You can't win

if you don't enter!
But then you can't win anyway, so enter-
tain the idea of going up and up and up,

trees taking measure of your hips then your heels
like a peasant flying through Chagall,
his sky turning from village blue

to the color of the winning ticket
in the lottery of love (which *is* love).
Here's to all of the above. You can't have

everything, but if you don't need anything
you're part way there. Nothing
will suffice, as one poet said,

and if your idea of luxury is on the level
of northern Wisconsin
you can smile

till the cows come home.
Bid them welcome,
they always do.

BLACKBERRIES

They lie
on the ground
after the deer
have left after the
bear has had her fill they

lie under the stars
and under the sun
in a cloud of brambles
the ripest ones
fall first
become black jam
in the thatch.

Late August, school
about to open, the aspen
would rattle in a saving breath
as a boy I hated
picking blackberries the
pail never full like
one half of a
slow
conversation.

Now
their taste
is sweeter
in memory
the insect buzz the
branches too high the blue
summer never quite
over before
the fall
begins.

THE LAKE

after Yeats

I'm getting up soon, and going to the lake,
where my father's cabin leans toward the north,
more chinks between the logs than last year's newsprint could patch,
old kitchen pots on the front room floor to catch the roof's leaks.

I'll catch black bass after dark in the lily pads,
and each day my father will talk about hunting birds this fall,
and my mother will read a book and occasionally
remember dreaming. It's a place of such anticipation

as when morning lifts its dew over the grass in August
and over blueberries too small in the wetlands, never grown sweet,
and the bittern standing on one leg, and the loon sane as day.
The mosquito buzz at evening sends us indoors—mostly safely

(everyone knows that joke, and the holes in the rusted screens).
Ok. I'm getting up now, because for days I've heard the frogs
awakening, and the blackbirds' fine syllables, and the few cars
on the road hidden behind the young red pines. I'm down that road,

away, always away now, and looking
toward its farthest bend.

Next to Nothing

it's the thing I want second most
the house next to the empty lot
the driftwood shelter on the world's last undeveloped beach
an efficiency apartment on the international space station

something very small, within

the words between ampersands
the friction between grains of sand
the time between maps

in the world outside metaphor
the one in which we think we mostly live
next to nothing you'll find that modest home
fenced yard, good light all day
east in the morning and west at suppertime

the place badly needs updating
that will take the rest of your life
just to think through

I want only four things and three of them are seasons
the last is light and darkness
it sounds extravagant at first

NOTES

"What Falls Away Is Always" is borrowed from "The Waking"
by Theodore Roethke:

> What falls away is always. And is near.
> I wake to sleep, and take my waking slow.
> I learn by going where I have to go.

"I like boring things" is a well-known line from Andy Warhol, drawn from
the poster for his first exhibition outside the United States.

The subheadings in "Diane Arbus," mostly captions, are borrowed from
Diane Arbus Revelations. The last lines of the poem are from Arbus's
writings.

"My life is not important..." is from "I'm Lucky" by Robert Dana,
published in *Starting Out for the Difficult World*.

"I think I could turn...," and the last two lines of the poem are from "Song
of Myself" by Walt Whitman.

"The Sense of Things Made Plain" is modeled after "The Plain Sense of
Things," by Wallace Stevens.

Every line in "Casablanca: The Stage Directions" comes from the
published screenplay.

Lines in "Becoming Groucho" that sound like Groucho Marx can be
found primarily in *Animal Crackers*.

"Fans, don't fail to miss tomorrow's game" is a line credited to Dizzy Dean
that I remember from my childhood. It appears in many books and
on many websites.

"The Villanelle is Hard to Master" is, of course, a parody of Elizabeth
Bishop's "The Art of Losing."

The *Hot-Blooded Dinosaurs* is by Adrian J. Desmond.

The line from Samuel Goldwyn appeared as a side bar in an issue of
   A View from the Loft, a magazine about craft circulated by the Loft
   Literary Center.

"Pissing in the snow..." is borrowed from *The Essential Haiku: Versions
   of Basho, Buson, & Issa* by Robert Hass.

"I'd like please..." is from "The Secret of Poetry" by Jon Anderson,
   published in *In Sepia*.

The lyrics to "These Foolish Things (Remind Me of You)" are by
   Eric Maschwitz.

"Like musical instruments..." is from "Poem" by Tom Clark, published
   most recently in *Sleepwalker's Fate: New and Selected Poems
   1965-1991*.

"The Lake" is modeled after "The Lake Isle of Innisfree" by W.B. Yeats.

About the Author

RICHARD TERRILL is the author of four previous books, including two poetry collections from the University of Tampa Press, *Almost Dark* (2010) and *Coming Late to Rachmaninoff* (2003), winner of the Minnesota Book Award. His memoirs are *Fakebook: Improvisations on a Journey Back to Jazz* (2000) and *Saturday Night in Baoding: A China Memoir* (1990), winner of the Associated Writing Programs Award for Nonfiction. He has been awarded fellowships from the National Endowment for the Arts, the Wisconsin and Minnesota State Arts Boards, the Jerome Foundation, the MacDowell Colony, and the Bread Loaf Writers' Conference, as well as Fulbright Fellowships to Korea, China, and Poland. Work has appeared in journals such as *Iowa Review*, *Georgia Review*, *North American Review*, *River Teeth*, *New Letters*, and *Crazyhorse*. He is Professor Emeritus at Minnesota State, Mankato, where he was a Distinguished Faculty Scholar, and currently works as a jazz saxophone player. He lives in Minneapolis.

For additional information, please visit *www.richardterrill.com*